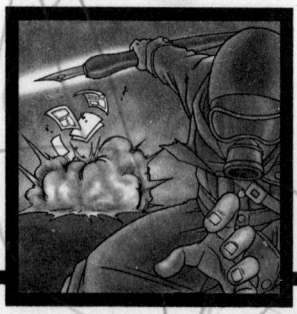

One time, after submitting a storyboard to Toriyama Sensei, he gave me this advice. He said, "What makes *Dragon Ball* so distinct and quirky is how it takes an ordinary concept or design and tweaks it ever so slightly."

Sensei... Isn't that the fundamental difference between a genius and a normal person...? Anyhow, I'm working hard to cross that divide!

—Toyotarou, 2018

Toyotarou

Toyotarou created the manga adaptation for the *Dragon Ball Z* anime's 2015 film, *Dragon Ball Z: Resurrection F*. He is also the author of the spin-off series *Dragon Ball Heroes: Victory Mission*, which debuted in *V-Jump* in Japan in November 2012.

Akira Toriyama

Renowned worldwide for his playful, innovative storytelling and humorous, distinctive art style, Akira Toriyama burst onto the manga scene in 1980 with the wildly popular *Dr. Slump*. His hit series *Dragon Ball* (published in the U.S. as *Dragon Ball* and *Dragon Ball Z*) ran from 1984 to 1995 in Shueisha's *Weekly Shonen Jump* magazine. He is also known for his design work on video games such as *Dragon Quest*, *Chrono Trigger*, *Tobal No. 1* and *Blue Dragon*. His recent manga works include *COWA!*, *Kajika*, *Sand Land*, *Neko Majin*, *Jaco the Galactic Patrolman* and a children's book, *Toccio the Angel*. He lives with his family in Japan.

SHONEN JUMP Manga Edition

STORY BY **Akira Toriyama**
ART BY **Toyotarou**

TRANSLATION **Toshikazu Aizawa, Christine Dashiell, and Caleb Cook**
LETTERING **Paolo Gattone and Chiara Antonelli**
TOUCH-UP ART **James Gaubatz**
DESIGN **Shawn Carrico**
EDITOR **Rae First**

DRAGON BALL SUPER © 2015 BY BIRD STUDIO, Toyotarou
All rights reserved. First published in Japan in 2015 by SHUEISHA Inc., Tokyo.
English translation rights arranged by SHUEISHA Inc.

The stories, characters and incidents mentioned in this publication are entirely fictional.

No portion of this book may be reproduced or transmitted in any form or by any means without written permission from the copyright holders.

Printed in the U.S.A.

Published by VIZ Media, LLC
P.O. Box 77010
San Francisco, CA 94107

10 9 8 7 6 5 4
First printing, May 2019
Fourth printing, September 2022

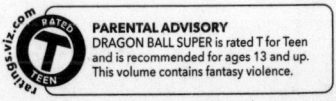

SHONEN JUMP MANGA

DRAGON BALL SUPER

THE DECISIVE BATTLE! FAREWELL, TRUNKS!

5

STORY BY
Akira Toriyama

ART BY
Toyotarou

CAST OF CHARACTERS

UNIVERSE 7

UNIVERSE 7: Future Parallel World

STORY THUS FAR

A long, long time ago, Son Goku left on a journey in search of the legendary Dragon Balls—a set of seven balls that, when gathered, would summon the dragon Shenlong to grant any wish. After a great adventure, he collects them all. Later, he becomes the apprentice of Kame-Sen'nin, fights a number of vicious enemies, defeats the great Majin Boo and restores peace on Earth. Some time passes, and then Lord Beerus, the God of Destruction, suddenly awakens and sets out in search of the Super Saiyan God. Goku, by becoming the Super Saiyan God, manages to stop Beerus from destroying the Earth and starts training under him with Vegeta. One day, future Trunks appears, hoping to save the future. Goku and Vegeta travel to the future with Trunks, but they soon find themselves struggling against Goku Black and the immortal Zamas of the parallel world. Goku's attempt to seal away Zamas with the Mafū-ba fails, and when he attempts to hit back, Goku Black and Zamas use the Potara Earrings to become the all-powerful God Zamas! Thrown from one brutal battle into the next, can Goku perfect Super Saiyan Blue in time?!

5

DRAGON BALL SUPER

EPISODE 25 **Will It be Goku?! Or Zamas?!** 07

EPISODE 26 **The Decisive Battle! Farewell, Trunks!** .. 53

EPISODE 27 **Life, Training and More** 99

EPISODE 28 **The Gods of Destruction from All 12 Universes** 145

DRAGON BALL SUPER

CHAPTER 25: WILL IT BE GOKU?! OR ZAMAS?!

GAH!!
HAH!!
WOOSH
ZOOM
BAM

BWSH
BRRBBL
THUNK
SWISH

GLARE
DASH
ZSH
BAH
!!

HOOM
DRAAAAH!!

THUD
DAMMIT ...!!
HAAAH!!
HAAH!...
HAAH!
GHHRRK
VOW

!!
BWOOM

GRRRRRSHHH

GAH!!

GOKU'S NOT PULLING HIS PUNCHES!
W-WHOA ...
BAM
BOOM

SMACK
BAM BAM BAM BAM
THM THM THM THM
WAM
GWAAH!
THWAK
HRRNGH!

STRIKE
THUD
ZSSH
THOOOM
RRMMM
!
...IMMOR-TAL!
I AM...
HUFF
HUFF
HUFF
HUFF
HUFF
HUFF
HUFF
HUFF

RRRIP

BURBL BURBL
HRAAH!!
KKRRKKK

I WON'T TAKE...
...ANY DAM-AGE!

AAAH...

!!

GAAH!
FWOOOSH
UGH!
THERE'S NO WAY...I'M LETTING YOU RECOVER NOW.
HUFF
HUFF
BAM
SSSHH
TCH... I DON'T HAVE MUCH TIME LEFT TO FIGHT LIKE THIS EITHER.
HE'S LOSING THE ABILITY TO CONTROL THE BLUE POWER WITHIN HIM.
WHAT?! REALLY?!
KAKAROT'S BODY IS PROBABLY ALREADY NEARING ITS LIMIT.
G-GOKU'S NOT LOOKING SO GOOD.

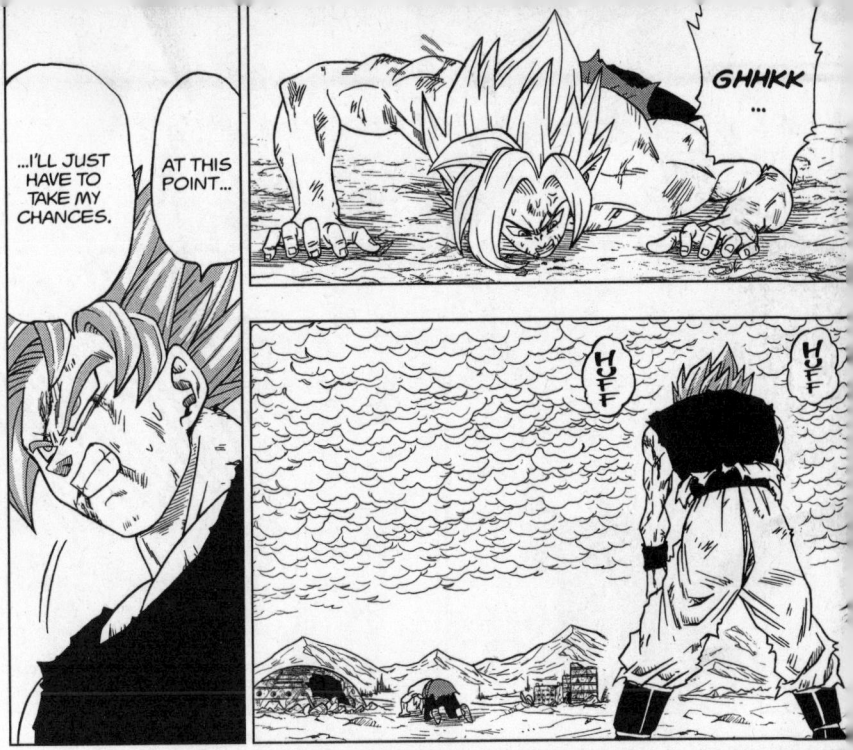
...I'LL JUST HAVE TO TAKE MY CHANCES.
AT THIS POINT...
GHHKK ...
HUFF
HUFF

HUFF
HUFF

HUFF
HUFF

FWSH
...THAT TECHNIQUE MIGHT JUST TAKE HIM DOWN.
EVEN IF HE'S IMMORTAL...
THIS IS HIS LAST CHANCE.
THERE WON'T BE A NEXT TIME.
B-BUT IF HE DOES THAT--
HE'S PLANNING TO RELEASE HIS REMAINING POWER WITH HIS NEXT ATTACK.
HUH? THERE'S A BLUE AURA AROUND GOKU'S FIST!
...!

YOU...
YOU...
I'M GOING TO WIPE YOU OUT ALONG WITH THIS WHOLE GALAXY !!
I DON'T NEED THIS COSMOS OR THE EARTH ANY-MORE!!
YOU SAIYAN SCUM!!
RAAAH!!!

BWOOOM
H-HE'S STILL GOT SO MUCH POWER LEFT!!
...
NO... NOT QUITE.
HE'S JUST LIKE KAKAROT.
HIS AURA'S POURING OUT FROM HIS INJURED BODY.
IF HE ALLOWS THAT MUCH ENERGY TO ERUPT WITHOUT FIRST RESTORING HIS PHYSICAL STAMINA--EVEN IF HE'S IMMORTAL--HE'LL STILL SUFFER THE CONSEQUENCES!
HE'S FLOWN INTO SUCH A RAGE THAT HE'S NO LONGER CONSIDERING THE BURDEN HE'S PUTTING ON HIMSELF.
DAAH!!

WOOO
THOOM
PSH
ZOOOM

GRIN
WHOOSH
ZIP

WHAT?!

SWISH

SORRY I GAVE THIS TECHNIQUE SUCH A BAD NAME, LORD BEERUS!
BUT I'LL BE USING IT NOW!!

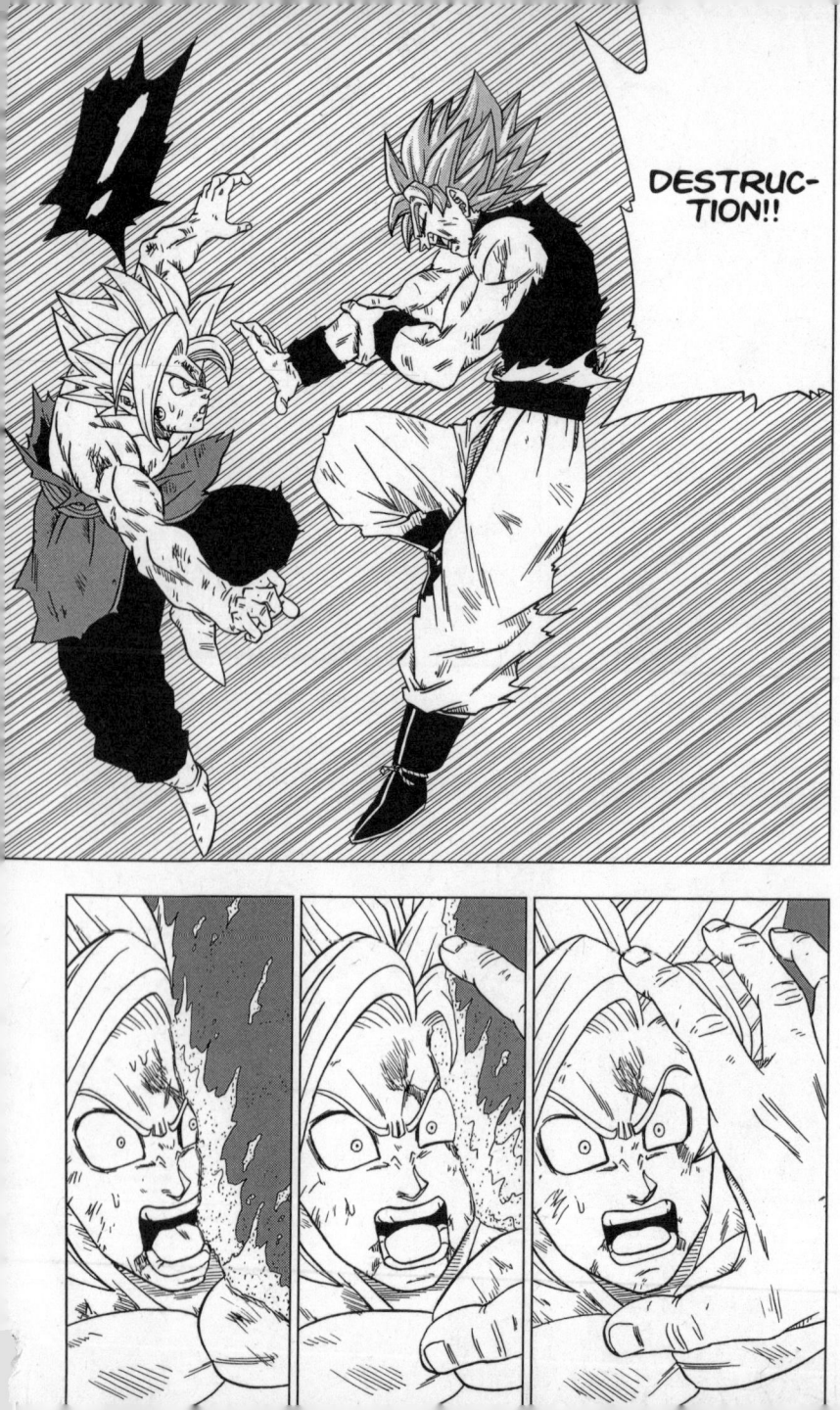
DESTRUC-
TION!!

GAH...
AH...
BEER-US'S TECH-NIQUE!
TH-THAT'S ...!!
GLINT
WHRRR
JAB

EEK!!
BLOOP
MAI!!
YANK
WHAT'RE YOU DOING?!
Y... YOU...
FLINCH

BASH
GAAH!!!
FWD
AAH! GOKU!!
TH-THAT IDIOT!!
THUD
SUFFL
SUFFL SUFFL

ZOOSH
IT'S A SHAME THAT A GOD WHO STANDS AT THE APEX OF ALL CREATION SHOULD WIN IN SUCH A SHAMEFUL WAY...!
NING
ZAMAS!!!!
...TO NEVER BOTHER WITH MORTALS AGAIN.
I'LL TAKE THIS AS A LESSON...

WHOOSH
WAAH!!!
BINEEN
BAM
DSSHH

THIS PLANET IS A PAIN. I'M GOING TO WIPE IT OUT.
NOW THEN.
...CREATING THEM AGAIN.
OR RATHER...
IT'S OVER.
IT'S...
AH...
AH... AH...

THADUMP

WRP

!
...

...!
SHF
TH-THIS MUST BE--

AN HOUR'S PASSED SINCE ZAMAS FUSED!!
IT'S BEEN AN HOUR.

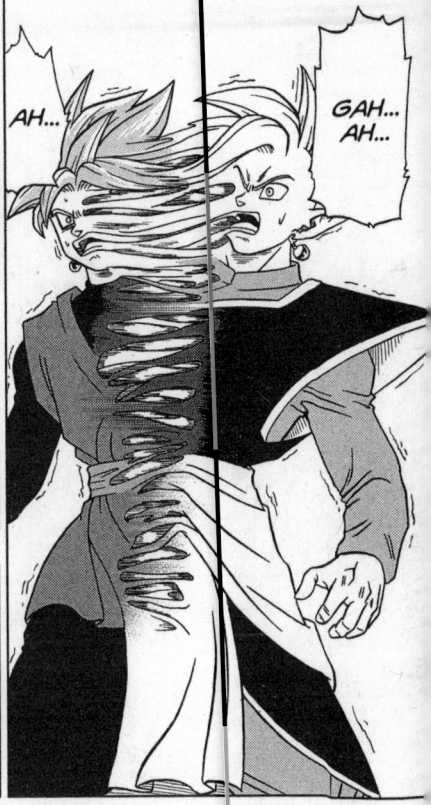
AH...
GAH... AH...

GWOOOOOO

?
...

GHHHH...
GHHHRKK...

OVER THE PAST HOUR, THEY MAY HAVE JOINED ON A CELLULAR LEVEL.
THOUGH WE CALL IT A FUSION, THEY'RE BOTH ZAMAS.
THEY'RE REJECTING...
...THE CANCELLATION ?!
BOTH ZAMASES ARE REJECTING THE SPLIT.
B-BUT THEY'RE SPLITTING DIFFERENTLY THAN GOKU AND VEGETA.
WHAT?!
WE ARE ONE...!
ONE GOD IS PLENTY ENOUGH.
GWOOO
I THOUGHT TIME WAS UP!
W-WHAT'S GOING ON?
I AM...THE ONE AND ONLY GOD.

ZA
SH

THUD
THUD

HUFF
HUFF
TRUNKS!!
!!!
THUNK
WSH!
RAAAAH!!!!
HUFF
HUFF

FWP
ZSH
N-NOW IT'S OVER...
BLACK.
TRUNKS FINISHED OFF GOKU BLACK!!

T-TRUNKS!

YOU DID IT.
YOU SAVED THE EARTH!
G...
GOKU.

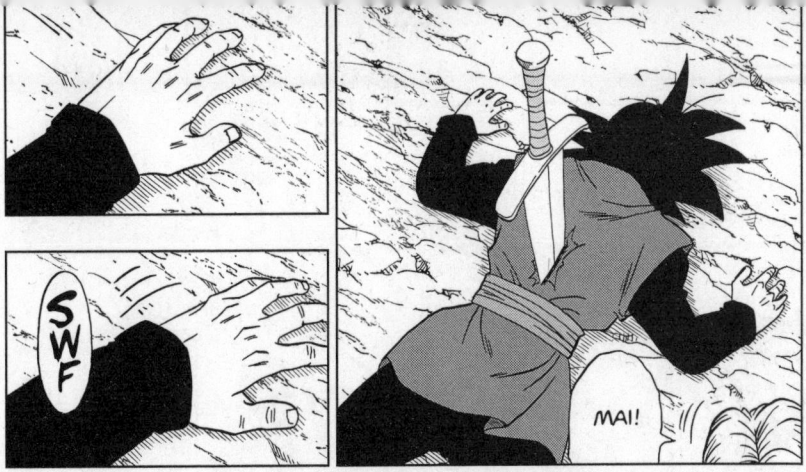
SWF
MAI!

GAAH!!!
BOOSH

THUD

!!

HUH?!

YOU...!
WHA--
...NOT SUP-POSED TO BE IMMOR-TAL...
YOU'RE...
KLTR
ZLSH
SNAP
GRAB

GLORP

WHAT?!

W-WHY DO YOU LOOK LIKE THAT?!

BUMP
!

Z-ZAMAS.

GLORP

H-HEY! YOU'VE GOT THE SAME FACE AS HIM!!

BASH
GWAH!
THERE ARE TWO FUSED ZAMAS-ES?!
IMPOS-SIBLE!

WAK
ZOOSH
KLANK
ROLL

GRP

D-DAMMIT. THEY'RE BOTH EQUALLY STRONG.
WHAT'S GOING ON HERE?!
HA HA HA...
TH-THIS COULDN'T GET ANY WORSE...
N-NOW THERE ARE TWO GOD ZAMASES!
SMAK
BASH

GUH ...
YOU... YOU...
BASTARDS!!
TRMBL TRMBL TRMBL
VEGETA...?

!
ZWOOOM
TH
UNK
HAAAH!!
BAM
VSSSHH

UUH...
V-VEGETA!
RRMMM
TAKE THIS!!
RRMMM
TNK
FWMP
TMP
GAMMA BURST!!

FLASH!!!!

PSSSHHH
FWAD
HUFF
HUFF
HUFF
HUFF

!
IT'S NO USE, VEGETA.
HE'LL ALWAYS REVIVE HIMSELF.
BLRP
BLRP
BLRP
TWCH
TWCH
BLORP
WRICL
WRICL
ZAMAS IS DISMEMBERED.
LAUNCHING A TECHNIQUE LIKE THAT WITH YOUR CURRENT STRENGTH...
YOU COULD'VE GOTTEN YOURSELF KILLED, DAD!!
HUFF
HUFF
FWP
FWP

WE CAN'T LEAVE ZAMAS LIKE THIS.
WHAT DO YOU MEAN RUN AWAY?
...
VEGE-TA! GOKU!
THIS IS OUR CHANCE TO RUN AWAY!
ZWOOSH
H-HOLD ON A SECOND!
HUH?!

WHY ARE THERE EVEN MORE OF HIM NOW?!

H-HEY. YOU, UM, GOT THE WRONG FACE ON.
WHAT?

DRAGON BALL SUPER

CHAPTER 26: THE DECISIVE BATTLE! FAREWELL, TRUNKS!

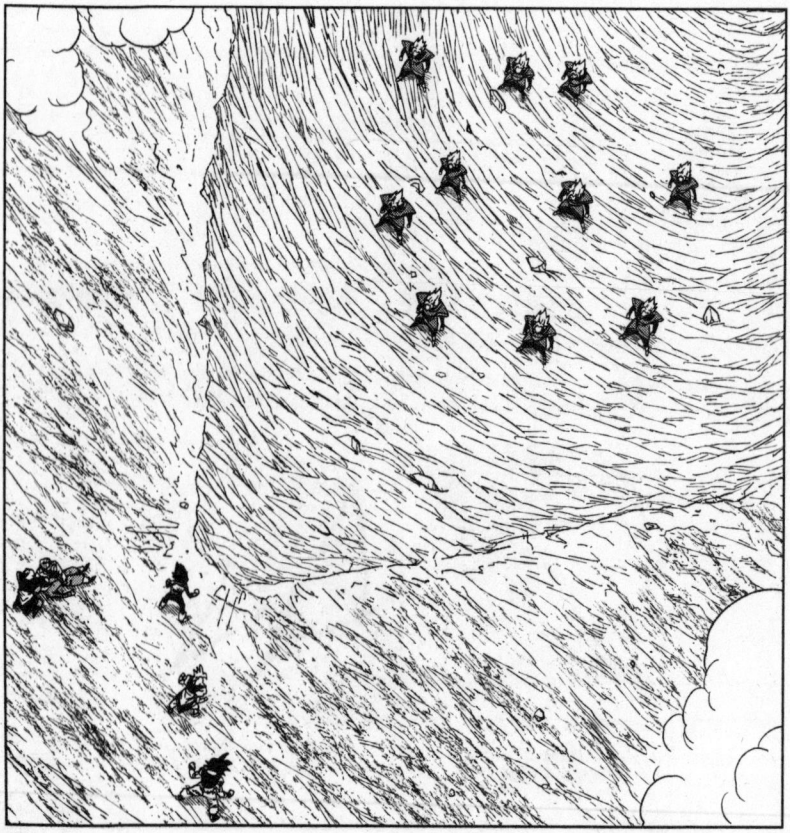

SKSH
SKSH

UGH ...
UH ...

VEGETA, TAKE MY HAND!!

TCH...

YOU TOO, GOKU. HURRY!
GRP

GIN OOO OOO !!

GRP
FWISH
FWISH

!
DUNDUNDUNDUNDUN
...

VWEEEN
PARALLEL WORLDS ARE NOT THE ONLY THING WE'RE GOING TO DESTROY!
GOWAS AND I WILL HEAD BACK WITH THE RING OF TIME. EVERYONE ELSE, GET IN THE TIME MACHINE!
TMP
1
CAPSULE CORP.
BUT ZAMAS SAID HE'S GONNA DESTROY THE REST OF THE PARALLEL WORLDS TOO!!
WE HAVE NO OTHER CHOICE!
ARE WE SERIOUSLY LEAVING WITH HIM STILL ALIVE?!
...!

SHF
SHF SHF SHF
ARE YOU TRYING TO ESCAPE WITH YOUR TIME MACHINE AGAIN?
SHF
SHF SHF
SHF
!
SHF
SHF

CAPSULE CORPORATION
WHO SAID WE'D USE THE RING OF TIME?
CHASE US?!
THAT'S CRAZY! YOU CAN'T USE THE RING OF TIME TO TRAVEL TO THE PAST!
THAT JERK...
TH-THERE ARE A LOT MORE OF THEM NOW!
I WON'T STOP CHASING YOU NO MATTER WHERE YOU GO!
PAST OR NOT, GO AHEAD AND RUN WHEREVER YOU WANT!

"LONG AGO, THERE WAS A HUMAN CIVILIZATION IN UNIVERSE 12 THAT POSSESSED HIGHLY SOPHISTICATED TECHNOLOGY. THEY INVENTED A DEVICE THAT COULD SEND A PERSON BACK IN TIME."
DAMMIT...!
!
WHAT DID HE SAY ?!!!
I HAVE A TIME MACHINE OF MY OWN!
THE ONE THAT WAS MADE IN UNIVERSE 12!
ZAMAS...TO THINK HE'D REMEMBER THAT!

TAP
THIS MEANS THAT THE ZERO MORTAL PROJECT CAN BE EXECUTED EVEN IN THE PAST!
THE LORD OF LORDS FROM UNIVERSE 12 WAS TAKING GOOD CARE OF IT.
THAT'S RIGHT! IT WAS YOU, GOWAS, WHO TOLD ME ABOUT IT.

...AND TERMINATE MANKIND THERE!
AND TO START, I SHALL VISIT THE WORLD WHERE YOU ALL CAME FROM...

TP TP TP TP

THAT IS ...
BUT ...

W-WHAT ...?!
!!

HOLD ON...
DOES THAT MEAN, EVEN IF WE ESCAPE, HE'LL JUST COME AFTER US?!

...
YOU MUST GIVE UP AND LET YOURSELF BE KILLED BY MY HANDS.
THAT'S RIGHT...
KAKAROT!
FATHER!! GOKU!!!
W-WHAT ARE YOU SAYING ?!!
THE REST OF YOU SHOULD GO BACK AND PRAY FOR A MIRACLE...
I'M STAYING HERE. I'LL FIGHT THEM OFF UNTIL THE END.
HMPH...
VEGETA...
...
!
IF YOU'RE STAYING, SO AM I.

AREN'T YOU GOING TO PROTECT THAT GIRL?
TRUNKS.

I CAN'T LEAVE YOU GUYS HERE!!
N-NO!!

YOU HEARD US, TRUNKS! JUST GO BACK TO THE PAST!

...!!

...
TAKE CARE OF BULMA.
NOW GO.
1
CAPSULE

DAM-MIT...
KLAK

UGH ...
TRUNKS. CLOSE THE HATCH BEFORE IT'S TOO LATE!

FATHER...

GWOO
VWEEM
1
CAPSULE CORP.
ALL RIGHT, VEGETA... YOU HAVE A PLAN?
OF COURSE NOT!
THEN LET'S DO THIS TO-GETHER.
I SEE...
THAT'S ALL.
GO WILD UNTIL YOU DIE.

HA!!!
HAA!!!
HWSH
HWSH
IF ONLY I HAD A SENZU BEAN WITH ME...
THIS IS FINE BY ME. AT LEAST I'LL GET TO SEE THE BIGGEST PAIN IN MY BUTT DIE...
I NEVER THOUGHT I'D MAKE MY LAST STAND LIKE THIS...
WISH I COULD GO CRAZY AS A SUPER SAIYAN, ESPECIALLY IN MY LAST BATTLE...
DARN... I DON'T HAVE AN OUNCE OF STRENGTH LEFT.
YOU SAID IT!
!
...
THIS IS...
HM?

HEY! KAIÔ-SHIN.
IS THE LORD OF EVERYTHING IN THIS TIMELINE STILL AROUND?
HUH?
HMM... THE LORD OF EVERY-THING?
I'M CERTAIN HE IS. NO ONE CAN DEFEAT THE LORD OF EVERY-THING.
WHY ARE YOU ASKING ME NOW?
YOU THINK THIS THING WILL WORK ON THE LORD OF EVERYTHING HERE?
!
TRUNKS! HOLD ON.
WE'RE ALL GOING BACK TO-GETHER!!
GOKU...
THAT'S ...!
WHAT?
WHAT'S HE SAYING ...?!
KLIK

FWIP

WHAT ?!!!!
!!

PAT
PAT
...!

...

THUD

...!
GAH!

THE L-LO...
TH-THAT IS...

THE LORD OF EVERY-THING ...!!!

MY NAME'S SON GOKU.
I'M A FRIEND OF YOURS IN A DIFFERENT TIMELINE.

ARE YOU THE ONE WHO CALLED ME?
WHO ARE YOU?

WHY IS THE LORD OF EVERY-THING HERE?!
W-WHY IS HE HERE?
!

...
HEY! ZENÔ-SAMA.

IT'S ALL MESSED UP.
WHAT'S THIS?
I SEE.
WURL
WURL
...!
...!
TH-THOSE GUYS DID ALL THIS...
THIS IS...
AH... THIS IS THE WORST!
IS THIS THEIR FAULT?
SO MANY OF THEM.
THEY ARE BAD GUYS.
Y-YES.

HOW ANNOY-ING.
RIGHT?
WHAT THE HECK IS HAPPENING DOWN THERE?!
WHAT THE?
YES, I THINK SO.
DON'T YOU WANT TO ERASE ALL OF THEM?

R-RUN ...!

W...
WORLD ?!!

A WORLD LIKE THIS...

TSK...
LORDS OF LORDS! YOU MUST HURRY AND GO BACK TOO!!
Y-YES.
THIS IS BAD!! VEGETA! GET IN THE TIME MACHINE!!
FWP
GO, TRUNKS !!!
GRP
GRP
WSH

DISAP-PEAR!
FWIP
SHWIP
KRAK
AH... AH...

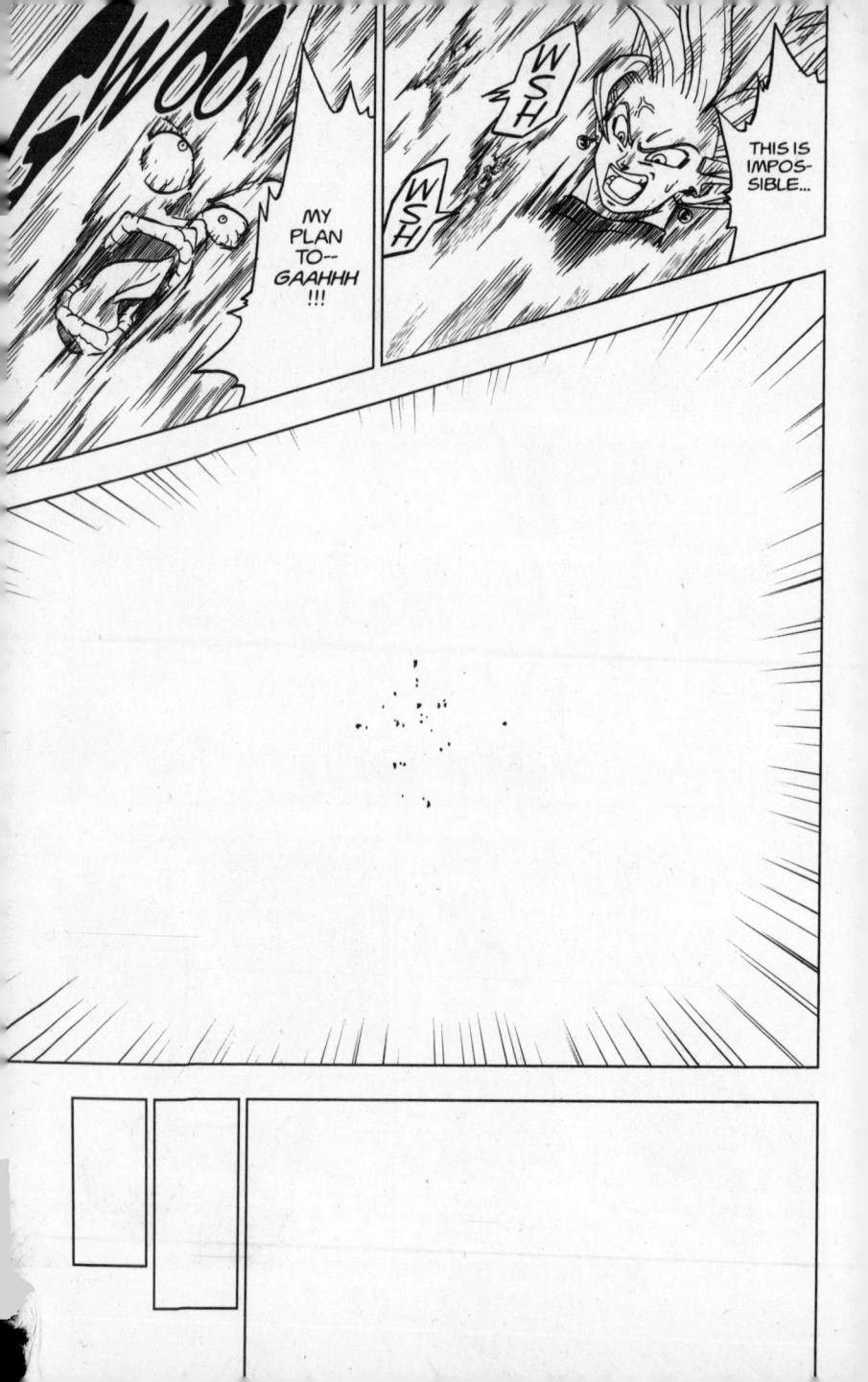
GWOO
MY PLAN TO-- GAAHHH !!!
WSH
WSH
THIS IS IMPOS-SIBLE...

KRAK
FSHH
MEOW
MEOW
MEOW
MEOW
?
TAP TAP TAP

PSHHH
PSHHH
VMM
I FEEL SICK...
UGHHH...
... BACK ...?
ARE WE...
IS EVERY-THING ALL RIGHT, GOKU ...?!!
UH...
OH MY...
KERPLUNK
VRRR

TRUNKS AND EVERY-ONE ARE BACK!!
CAPSUL

C.C. AIR FORCE

HUG
BMF

SHOOM

BWOO
THANKS, KIBITO!
PHEW ...

STILL... I WOULD SAY IT'S BETTER THAN LOSING EVERY-THING ...

YES, THE LORD OF EVERY-THING DE-STROYED IT ALONG WITH ZAMAS...
AFTER ALL, TRUNKS'S FUTURE IS GONE FOREVER.
...

YES... I WON-DER WHAT HAP-PENED TO US...
HEY, SHU... LOOKS LIKE MAI WAS THE ONLY ONE OF US LEFT IN THE FUTURE.

IT SEEMS YOU'RE DOING GREAT...
OH... YOU'VE GROWN UP...

SHU!
PILAF!

MAI, I MEAN THE BIG ONE!
HEY!

YOU SHOULD GREET HIM!
LORD BEERUS HAS ARRIVED.
HMM, THERE'S SOMETHING I WANT TO ASK YOU...
Y-YES, BUT...
YOU TOO, PILAF. YOU LOOK LIKE YOU'RE DOING WELL YOURSELF!
MAI!
IN THE FUTURE, ARE WE...
I BET YOUR POWER WASN'T GOOD ENOUGH TO DEFEAT HIM AFTER ALL.
HMPH...I CAN TELL YOU HAD A REALLY HARD TIME.
BEERUS! WE MANAGED TO DEFEAT ZAMAS!
HE IS THE GOD OF DESTRUCTION FROM UNIVERSE 7.
LORD BEERUS?
NOW, TELL ME EVERYTHING THAT HAPPENED.
HA HA HA...I KNEW YOU WOULD SAY THAT.

GAB
GAB
WAH
WAH
SIZZL

I GET IT. THEY ARE THE PERFECT MATCH...
SIGH ...

THANKS!
TRUNKS, YOU TRY THIS TOO!

YOU SHOULD TRY THAT.
RIGHT ?
I CAN'T BELIEVE IT. THIS IS SO GOOD...

YOUR SINS MAKE ME SPEECH-LESS!
YOU EVEN MADE USE OF THE LORD OF EVERY-THING AT THE END...

YOU DAMN FOOL! YOU ALMOST GOT ME KILLED!
WHAT?! YOU WENT TO THE FUTURE TOO, KAIÔ-SHIN...?!
I FEEL SO STUPID... I'M DONE HERE.

YOU ALMOST GOT US KILLED TOO.
THAT WAS THE ONLY THING I COULD THINK OF.
THOUGH I DIDN'T THINK HE'D DESTROY THE ENTIRE UNIVERSE.
YES...
RIGHT... IN THE END, TRUNKS'S FUTURE IS GONE...
STILL, WE MANAGED TO DEFEAT ZAMAS.
AND WE PROTECTED THE REST OF THE PARALLEL WORLDS-- IT WASN'T THE WORST OUTCOME.
WELL, HAVING TOO MANY PARALLEL WORLDS IS NEVER A GOOD THING.
YOU'RE RIGHT. PERHAPS IT WAS GOOD SINCE YOU PUT THE PARALLEL WORLDS IN ORDER!
...
THAT'S WHAT I THOUGHT AT FIRST, BUT...
YOU'VE GOTTA BE KIDDING!!
DO YOU EVEN REALIZE THAT THESE TWO HAVE NO PLACE TO GO BACK TO ANYMORE?!
HUH?
DIDN'T YOU SAY WE COULDN'T GO BACK THERE ANYWAY, RIGHT?

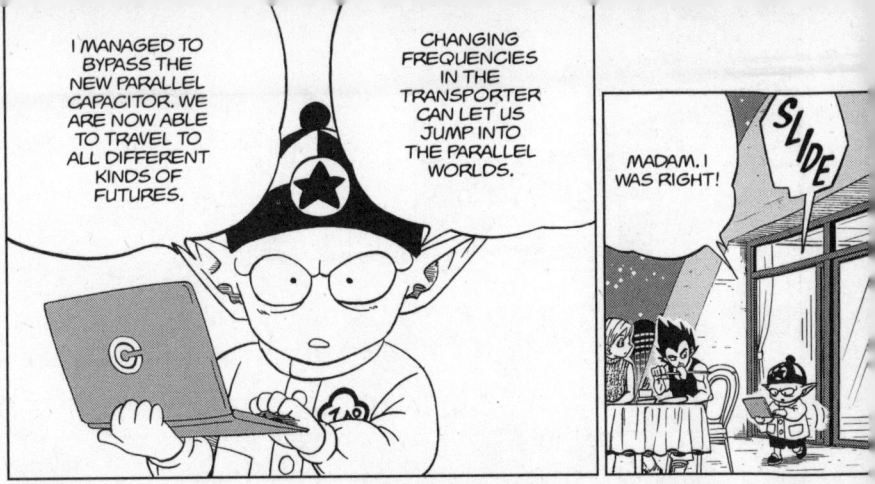
I MANAGED TO BYPASS THE NEW PARALLEL CAPACITOR. WE ARE NOW ABLE TO TRAVEL TO ALL DIFFERENT KINDS OF FUTURES.
CHANGING FREQUENCIES IN THE TRANSPORTER CAN LET US JUMP INTO THE PARALLEL WORLDS.
MADAM. I WAS RIGHT!
SLIDE

I DIDN'T KNOW YOU WERE THIS SMART...
I STILL HAVE A LONG WAY TO GO...
YOU HEARD HIM...

WHAT FOR? YOU DON'T NEED THAT ANY-MORE.
CAN YOU REFUEL THE TIME MACHINE FOR ME?
BULMA !

AH!

THESE JERKS... THEY JUST KEEP IGNORING THE RULES OF THE UNIVERSE!
LET'S JUST PRETEND WE DIDN'T SEE IT THIS TIME, BEERUS. YOU'RE STILL ALIVE THANKS TO THEM.

PLEASE !!
I REALLY DO, ACTU-ALLY.

SHOOM
WHAT'S IT LIKE? CAN YOU SEE ANYTHING?
THERE HE IS!
ZENÔ-SAMA!
AH!
SON GOKU.
EVERY-THING'S GONE.
THEN I'LL TAKE YOU TO SOMEWHERE THAT'S MORE FUN!
REALLY?

HI!
HERE IT IS.

VMM

ZENÔ-SAMA... THIS TIME...
KAIÔ-SHIN...

ZENÔ-SAMA...
Z... ZE...

PAY YOUR RESPECTS !!!
YOU FOOL!!!!

I WANT YOU TO TAKE US TO HIM NOW.

...!

...
...

HEY, ZEN-CHAN!
AH, GOKU!

JUST AS PROM-ISED, I BROUGHT YOU A NEW FRIEND.

YES.
LET'S PLAY.

HI.
HI.

WAH!
WAH!

WHIS, WAS THIS YOUR IDEA?
NO, IT WAS ALL HIS DOING.

IT ALL WORKED OUT.
HEH HEH HEH ...

I WILL. ONE DAY.

FATHER.
YOU CAN COME VISIT US ANY-TIME.

IT MAKES ME EN-VIOUS OF UNI-VERSE 7.
I SEE.

THANK YOU FOR YOUR HELP. I MUST RETURN TO UNIVERSE 10.
I TRULY APOLOGIZE FOR THE TROUBLE I BROUGHT TO ALL OF YOU.
I UNDERSTAND...
BE CAREFUL WHO YOU ADOPT AS AN APPRENTICE NEXT TIME.
SHM
WELL, THEN.
LET'S GO, WHIS.
YES!
チョコレート
Chocolate
クッキー
THANK YOU, BUT WE'VE MADE OUR DECISION.
HE'S RIGHT.
WHAT? I DON'T KNOW YET... YOU SHOULD JUST STAY HERE WITH US.
...IS IT STILL POSSIBLE FOR US TO GO TO THE TIME BEFORE ZAMAS AND DABRA SHOW UP?
WE ALSO WANT TO GO BACK TO THE FUTURE, BUT...
MOM.
SuperDB

OH, BUT YOU ALSO MADE ANOTHER ONE.
WHIS! DON'T DO ANYTHING STUPID! YOU'RE GOING TO CREATE ANOTHER PARALLEL WORLD!
IS THAT TRUE?!
OF COURSE IT'S POSSIBLE.
HRMM...

...IF ZAMAS SHOWS UP AGAIN, HE MIGHT COME KILL YOU!
YOU CAN'T! I'M NOT SURE ABOUT THIS DABRA GUY, BUT...

HO HO HO. WE HAVE SOMETHING MORE CONVENIENT THAN THE LITTLE JAR THAT YOU BROUGHT WITH YOU.
DON'T YOU DARE UNDER-ESTIMATE THE GOD OF DESTRUC-TION!

WHAT? I SEE...
THEN HOW'D YOU DO IT?

YOU SHOULD TALK TO THE LORD BEERUS ON THE OTHER SIDE AND HE'LL GIVE YOU A HAND.
IF I MANAGE NOT TO GET KILLED BY DABRA, LORD BEERUS WON'T DIE EITHER.

WHY DIDN'T YOU GUYS TELL ME?!
WHAT ...?!

NO... I CAN'T KILL IMMOR-TALS...
OH, SO YOU HAVE A TECHNIQUE THAT CAN KILL IMMORTALS?

ONLY THIS TIME, I'LL LET IT PASS.
Y-YES...
SuperDB
COME ON...
STOP WHINING. THAT'S PART OF YOUR TRAIN-ING.
TCH...
TRUNKS.
BUT PLEASE REMEMBER, YOU'LL HAVE TO SEE ANOTHER TRUNKS AND MAI LIVING THERE. ARE YOU SURE YOU'RE FINE WITH THAT?
TH-THANK YOU, MY LORD.
FINE. DO AS YOU WISH.
SO, YOU REALLY LEAVING?
YEAH... HAVING TWO OF US WILL DOUBLE THE POWER.
THAT'S FINE.
RIGHT ...
SuperDB

MAKE IT COUNT.
LET'S GO, WHIS.
SHM
YEAH.
SuperDB
I WILL!

THANK YOU.
LORD BEER-US.
SuperDB

WOOSH

ARE YOU SURE YOU WANT TO LEAVE? IF YOU LIKE, I COULD ADOPT YOU AS MY APPRENTICE AND BOTH OF YOU COULD LIVE TOGETHER IN OUR SACRED WORLD.
TAKE THIS CAPSULE SET WITH YOU. THERE'S FOOD AND OTHER NECESSITIES IN IT.
TWO DAYS LATER..
THANK YOU.
1
CAPSULE CORP.

I UNDERSTAND...

I'VE NEVER BEEN IN SUCH A LUXURIOUS POSITION, WHICH IS WHY I'M GOING TO WITHDRAW FROM YOUR APPRENTICESHIP ONCE I DEFEAT BOBIDDI AND DABRA.
I APPRECIATE YOUR OFFER, MY LORD. BUT THE ONLY REASON I BECAME YOUR APPRENTICE WAS TO DESTROY BOBIDDI-- IT WAS ONLY TEMPORARY.

PLEASE SAY HI TO ME ON THE OTHER SIDE.
I WILL.
HMMM... I DON'T REALLY GET WHAT'S GOING ON...

IT'S HIS WAY OF SETTLING THINGS.
THAT'S NOT THE POINT.
HEY...IF HE QUITS THE APPRENTICESHIP, DOESN'T THAT MEAN HE WON'T BE ABLE TO USE HIS HEALING POWERS ANYMORE? ISN'T THAT A WASTE?

I PROMISE.
YOU'RE RIGHT.
YEAH.
ME FROM THE FUTURE! MAKE SURE HE MAKES YOU HAPPY!
!
YEAH.
BIG BRO! COME VISIT US SOMETIME!

YEAH RIGHT. AT FIRST I THOUGHT HE WAS COOL, BUT I DON'T THINK I CAN CATCH UP WITH THAT SERIOUS ATMOSPHERE.
I THOUGHT YOU HAD A CRUSH ON HIM...
MAI, ARE YOU OKAY WITH THAT?

PLUS, LOOKS LIKE I ONLY HAVE TO WAIT A WHILE FOR YOU TO LOOK COOL LIKE HIM...
WHAT ?!
OH WELL. FOR NOW, I THINK I LIKE YOU BEST.

SERIOUS ATMOSPHERE?

...SHE'S SAID SHE LIKES ME...
THIS IS THE FIRST TIME...

YOU ARE A MAN OF THE FUTURE. YOU MAY NOT BE ABLE TO REGAIN YOUR LOST TIMELINE, BUT IF THERE'S A CHANCE TO CREATE A WHOLE NEW PEACEFUL ONE, YOU'LL DO IT!
TRUNKS! I'M NOT SMART ENOUGH TO UNDERSTAND DIFFICULT THINGS, BUT I'M SURE YOUR DECISION IS THE RIGHT ONE.
FAREWELL, EVERYONE!
DON'T SLACK OFF ON YOUR TRAIN-ING.
GET STRON-GER, TRUNKS.
...
SAY HI TO YOUR MOM ON THE OTHER SIDE!
ANYWAYS, JUST BE HAPPY!
GOKU...
EVERYONE ELSE TOO-- THANK YOU FOR YOUR HELP.
YES, FATHER!
...!

FARE-WELL, EVERY-ONE!
VMMM
TO THINK THAT YOU'LL END UP LIKE THAT...
WHEEEN
WHAT? WHAT EXACTLY DOES HAPPEN?
AH... RIGHT... YOU DON'T KNOW WHAT'S WAITING FOR YOU...
SHP
MAI! TELL ME ONE LAST TIME!
WHAT HAP-PENED TO ME IN THE FU-TURE?

VMM
GOODBYE!
IT WAS NICE SEEING YOU TOO, PILAF!
WAIT UP, MAI!!
TELL ME WHAT HAPPENS IN THE FUTURE!

YOU'LL BE JUST FINE WITHOUT US.
GOOD LUCK... TRUNKS!
J-JUST WHAT HAPPENS TO ME IN THE FUTURE?!

ALL TO SAVE MY FUTURE SELF! GET READY FOR THE FUTURE PILAF ARC!
MAKING HIS OWN TIME MACHINE.
WHAT'S PILAF UP TO?

DRAGON BALL SUPER

CHAPTER 27: LIFE, TRAINING AND MORE

UNIVERSE 7, EARTH...

...EVERY-ONE'S LIVES CON-TINUE PEACE-FULLY...
OBLIVIOUS TO THE INTENSE BATTLE WITH ZAMAS...

SEE YOU AROUND!
THANKS. HAVE A GOOD DAY.

TAP

VWEEEM
VWEEEM
LA♪ LA DEE DEE DA DA ♫
AND IN A BACK-WATER TOWN LIKE THIS...
OH? ISN'T THAT THE LATEST AIR TRUCK MODEL?
YEAH...
NEED HELP?

NO PROBLEM. HOP IN!
CAN I HITCH A RIDE TO THE NEAREST STATION?
THANKS!

GET OUT OF THE TRUCK AND SCRAM!
HEY, YOU!
HA HA HA...

GUESS IT'S OUR LUCKY DAY!
LOOK AT THAT TRUCK! YOU DON'T SEE SUCH FANCY MODELS AROUND HERE.

BAN-DITS?
I DON'T THINK IT'S A GOOD IDEA TO TAKE BANDITS TO THE STATION...

WE'RE BANDITS.
THAT TRUCK'S OURS NOW!

HUH?
WHAT...?

OH! SO YOU'RE TRYING TO STEAL IT?
IS THIS GUY AN IDIOT?
NO! WE ALREADY TOLD YOU WE'RE TAKING YOUR TRUCK! GIVE ME THE KEY ALREADY!
YOU FINALLY GET IT!
THAT'S RIGHT!
AWE-SOME!
WE'VE HIT THE JACKPOT! WE'RE GONNA BE RICH!
BOSS, CHECK THIS OUT! THIS GULL WING IS THE NEWEST MODEL!
OH!
...
HA HA HA!
HEE HEE HEE!
GYA HA HA!
TODAY'S OUR LUCKY DAY!

HMPH! YOU DON'T UNDERSTAND THE SITUATION HERE AT ALL.
WHAT AN IDIOT!
LET ME TEACH YOU WHAT HAPPENS...
...WHEN YOU TRY TO GO AGAINST US.
BULMA GAVE ME THIS TRUCK SO I'D WORK HARDER.
I CAN'T AFFORD TO GIVE IT TO YOU GUYS.
HM...?
WHAT'S SO FUNNY?
TAP
TAKE THIS !!!!
SHOOM
!
!
!

FWIP
WOOSH
THUNK

YOU...
...BASTARD!!
KLAK

UGH...
!
B-BOSS!!

FWIP
BLAM BLAM BLAM BLAM BLAM

THUD
CRAP!!

SHOOP
THAK

GRP
!!

TMP
GYAH...

SNAP
!

AH...
I GUESS I'M NOT ONE TO TALK...
GO GET A JOB INSTEAD OF PULLING STUNTS LIKE THIS!
I'LL SHOW YOU...
DIE!!!
BAMBAMBAM
!
FWIP FWIP FWIP FWIP FWIP

HE'S A MON-STER !!!
OH NO!
GAH!
FLK
FLK

WHAT SHOULD I DO?
SHOOT... HE LEFT HIS BUDDIES BEHIND...

BUT I PROMISED CHI-CHI THAT I'D WORK...
I SHOULD GET BACK TO TRAINING...

LOOKS LIKE I'M GETTING OUT OF SHAPE...
HUH?

OF COURSE! THESE TWO ARE WANTED CRIMINALS WITH A BOUNTY ON THEIR HEADS!
YOU SURE I CAN HAVE THIS MUCH?
OOOH!
POLICE
HEY, WHIS!
IT'S THE COMMUNICATION DEVICE I GOT FROM WHIS!
HERE IT IS...
POLICE
THANKS, MAN!
I'M SURE CHI-CHI WILL LET ME GO BACK TO TRAINING IF I SHOW HER ALL THIS MONEY!
ALL RIGHT!
YOU IN BED? COME ON! I NEED TO GET BACK TO TRAINING.
CAN YOU HEAR ME?
YO?
HE'S NOT RESPONDING...
...
SHHHH

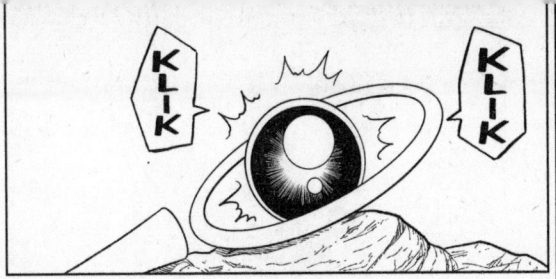
KLIK
KLIK

RAH!
HA!
KLIK
KLIK

SHF
SHF

TAKE THIS!!
FWIP
FWIP

POW POW POW POW

YOU'RE GETTING BETTER, VEGETA.
YOUR MOVES ARE GETTING SHARPER.
YAWN!
I'M BORED.
HRAH!!!
!
BWF

...
PLIP
FWD
GWOO

GRP
CORRECT.
SHUP
I GOT YOU!!!
I DON'T NEED YOUR COMPLIMENTS!
HMPH!
GRAH!
HA!
...
YOU'VE GROWN AS A WARRIOR, VEGETA.
YOU DID WELL.
I'M GOING TO BED.
OKAY, THIS IS ENOUGH.
TUP
¡IT'S A STUPID RIVALRY--NOT WORTH MY TIME.
AH ...
IT MUST BE BECAUSE SON GOKU WAS STRONGER THAN HIM DURING THE BATTLE WITH ZAMAS.
HE'S MORE INTO THIS THAN USUAL ...
WHAT'S UP WITH HIM?

THEY'LL BE YOUR STRONGEST RIVALS.
THEY WILL.

YOUR PROPHESY THAT THEY WOULD BECOME MY STRONGEST RIVALS WAS EXAGGERATED AFTER ALL.
YAWN!

...

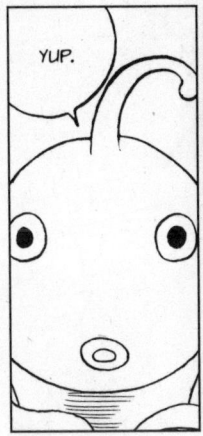
YUP.

MY RIVALS?

YUP.

THOSE TWO?

HEY! VEGETA!
FSHH

TCH...
...

OH, LORD BEERUS.
I THOUGHT YOU WERE TAKING A BREAK.
...
I CAN TELL YOU'VE MADE A LOT OF PROGRESS.
!
SO...HOW ABOUT WE GO AT IT AGAIN?
I'VE CHANGED MY MIND.
...
YOU SHOULD DO IT, VEGETA.
HOW UNUSUAL.
WHAT?
I AC-CEPT.
VERY WELL...

HRAH!!!!
HWOOSH

AH...SO THAT'S WHY.

I'M NOT THE SAME AS I WAS BEFORE ...

IT'S BEEN A FEW YEARS ...

YUP. I SAID THOSE TWO SAIYANS WILL BECOME HIS RIVALS ONE DAY.
BY ANY CHANCE, DID YOU SAY SOMETHING TO BEERUS?

SUPER SAIYAN BLUE...
BSH
BWSH

BRING IT ON...
...VEGE-TA.
THOOOM

FWP
HOWEVER, YOUR TRANSFORMATION IS JUST A MERE POWER-UP FROM SUPER SAIYAN GOD--THAT'S NOT ENOUGH TO REACH MY LEVEL.
MY HAND EVEN SHOOK A BIT.
I SEE... THE MOMENT OF IMPACT WAS INDEED MAGNIFICENT.
GRAH !!!!
TMP
TMP

BOOM
EAT THIS !!!!
SHM
SWAP
SWSH

HRAAAAH!!!!
DAMMIT!
FSHIFSHIFSH!
DAH!!!

SWF
BWOOSH
WHP

WHRL
DSH
FEH...
TP
GW

KRASH
!!
HMPH ...
SPLASH
BURBL
BURBL
HM...? THAT WAS SURPRISINGLY QUICK...

FSHHH
FSH
BZZT
BZZT
WANNA GO AGAIN?
WHAT'S THIS?
?
SST

PHEW...

SSHHH

IF KAKAROT CAN DO IT, SO CAN I!

OOOH ?

VEGETA. THAT'S THE SAME FORM GOKU USED! WHEN DID YOU LEARN HOW TO DO THAT?

LET'S CONTINUE!
HEE HEE HEE... THIS IS EXCITING !

SHF
WAK
THUD

BWO
WORL
TAKE THAT !!
...
OOM
FWIP
FWIP

YOU'VE IM-PROVED A BIT!
BUT I WONDER HOW LONG YOU'LL LAST...
WSH
FWIP
SWH
GLARE
FWIP
SHOOM
POW
POW
POW
POW
POW
HWK THWK

BAM
BAMBAMBAM
HRAAAAH!!!
TCH...

BUT I BELIEVE IT'S ABOUT TIME HE GOT SERIOUS. IT WOULD BE TROUBLESOME IF HE GOT HIT AND LOST HIS TEMPER...
NO. HE'S STILL PLAYING AROUND.
I DON'T WANT THAT EITHER. HE'S UNPREDICTABLE WHEN HE'S ANGRY...

BAM BAMBAM
THOOM
I SUPPOSE GOKU IS NO LONGER AHEAD OF HIM.
IT APPEARS VEGETA HAS COMPLETE CONTROL OVER SUPER SAIYAN BLUE.
IS BEERUS FIGHTING SERIOUSLY?

!

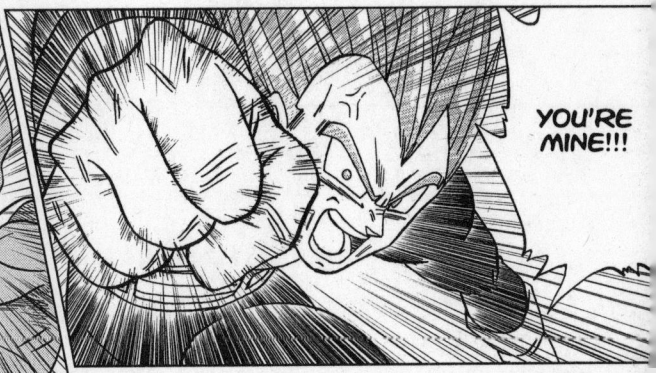
YOU'RE MINE!!!

GOT YOU!
...
AH!
OH!
...
HE DID IT!
HE SURE DID.

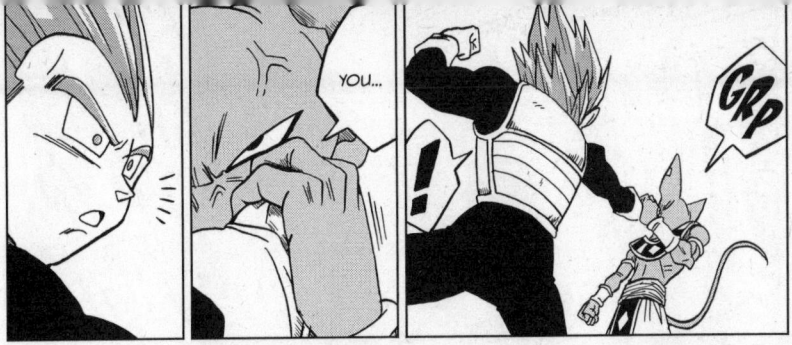
YOU...
!
GRP

DON'T GET COCKY.
SKWEEZ

OH?
DID I DROP MY SCEPTER SOME-WHERE...?

WILL DO.
SHF
WHIS! CREATE A BARRIER BEFORE HE GETS OUT OF CONTROL!

!

HEY!!!

!
!
FLASH

BOO——OM

GOOD-NESS... THAT WAS BIG...

DAM-MIT...

YOU GOT CARRIED AWAY WHILE I WAS GOING EASY ON YOU...
GAH...

AT THIS RATE, IT'LL TAKE YOU A MILLION YEARS TO BECOME MY RIVAL!

TAP
WHIS, FIX THIS MESS.
AS YOU WISH.

WELL...I'LL GIVE YOU POINTS FOR IMPROVING SO QUICKLY.
YOU COULD PROBABLY BE A CANDIDATE FOR A GOD OF DESTRUC-TION IN ANOTHER UNIVERSE...

YOU DID VERY WELL.
YOU DON'T HAVE TO FEEL THE STING OF DEFEAT, VEGETA.
DAMN ...
TP
AFTER ALL, YOUR OPPONENT IS THE GOD OF DESTRUCTION OF THIS UNIVERSE.
WHAT DID YOU EXPECT?
I'M NO MATCH FOR HIM AT ALL...
DOING THAT IS LIMITING. IT WILL TAKE SOME TIME FOR YOUR BRAIN AND SENSES TO GET YOUR BODY TO MOVE HOW YOU WANT.
I CAN TELL THAT YOU STILL THINK FIRST AND MOVE LATER.
...THAT'S WHAT YOU'RE SAYING, RIGHT ?
ONCE I MASTER IT, I'LL BE ABLE TO TAKE ON ANY ENEMY...
EVEN LORD BEERUS HASN'T MASTERED IT.
YOU MUST BE ABLE TO LET EVERY SINGLE PART OF YOUR BODY JUDGE AND ACT ON ITS OWN.
INDEED.
AND THAT'S VERY DIFFICULT.

KAKAROT AND I ARE EQUALS. BUT WE ARE FAR FROM REACHING OUR FULL POTENTIAL.
?

THAT MEANS... I STILL HAVE A LONG WAY TO GO.

AS LONG AS I KNOW THAT, THAT'S ALL I NEED.
...

I'M SICK OF FOLLOWING AFTER HIM.
I'M THE ONE WHO WILL GET TO THE TOP FIRST.

?
SORRY, BUT I NEED YOU TO TAKE ME BACK TO EARTH.
IS SOME-THING WRONG?

WELL THEN, STARTING TOMORROW, SHALL I INCREASE YOUR TIME FOR TRAINING?
NO. I'LL SAVE THE NEXT SESSION FOR ANOTHER TIME.

SO THAT'S WHAT YOU WERE REFER-RING TO.
I SEE.

KLIK
KLIK
SOMEONE WAS TRYING TO REACH YOU.
HEEEY, WHIS!
FOR A WHILE?
I WON'T BE COMING BACK HERE FOR QUITE A WHILE.
I FOUND YOUR SCEPTER.
I WONDER WHO'S CALLING ME.
AH, YES.
WHIS, IT'S ME! GOKU!
THERE YOU ARE!
HELLO? WHO ARE YOU??
DAIFUKU?! IT SOUNDS BOLD YET SCRUMPTIOUS.
IT'S REALLY DELICIOUS AND CLASSY!
THAT'S FINE... SO, WHAT ARE YOU BRINGING ME THIS TIME?
I GOT SOME DAIFUKU FOR YOU!
IT'S BEEN A WHILE, BUT I WANTED TO ASK YOU TO TRAIN ME AGAIN!
HOW CAN I HELP YOU?
OH, GOKU!

CAPSULE CO
INFORMATION
CAN WE MEET UP HERE IN AN HOUR?
I'M AT BULMA'S RIGHT NOW. I THOUGHT WE COULD INVITE VEGETA TOO.

BUT VEGETA'S ABOUT TO LEAVE...
WHAT? HOW COME?

HUH?!
THAT'S CHEATING! HE WAS TRAINING WITHOUT ME?! LET ME JOIN YOU GUYS THEN!

OH? VEGETA'S ALREADY HERE WITH ME.

IT'S ALMOST TIME FOR IT TO BE BORN...
...

WHY ARE YOU LEAVING, VEGETA?

THANKS FOR COMING TO SEE ME!
DUUN
SORRY I KEPT YOU WAITING! WELCOME BACK, GOKU!
HUH? A BIRTH?
YOU'RE EATING TOO MUCH!
WHAT'S UP WITH THAT BELLY?
OH BOY...
HA HA HA!
SO HE WAS TALKING ABOUT YOUR BABY, HUH?
HUH? OH, RIGHT. YEAH, YOU DID SAY SOMETHING ABOUT THAT.
I TOLD YOU AREADY-- I'M EXPECT-ING A SECOND KID!
WHAT?! SO YOU CAME HERE FOR SOMETHING ELSE?

BOOM

ONE HOUR LATER ...
VWEEM

NOW, LET'S GET GOING.
THANKS FOR WAITING.

HEY, WHIS!

HOW STUPID ARE YOU?! IF I LEAVE TO GO TRAIN NOW, SHE'LL NEVER FORGIVE ME!
WHY? YOU'RE NOT THE ONE GIVING BIRTH.

CAN'T YOU TELL BY LOOKING AT BULMA? SHE'S GONNA GIVE BIRTH ANY DAY NOW, AND I NEED TO STAY WITH HER.
VEGETA, WHY'RE YOU LEAVING?

LOOK AT ME! I DON'T EVEN KNOW WHEN GOHAN AND GOTEN WERE BORN.
WHY DO YOU CARE?!

YOU MAY NOT BE A BAD PERSON...
...BUT YOU'RE A HORRIBLE FATHER.
HUH?
DON'T BLAME ME IF I GET WAY STRONGER THAN YOU, OKAY?
JUST GO ALREADY!
MAYBE I'M NOT FAMILIAR ENOUGH WITH EARTH CUSTOMS TO UNDERSTAND THIS...
ANYWAY, LET'S GET GOING, SHALL WE?
BY THE WAY, DO YOU HAVE THAT DELICACY CALLED DAIFUKU WITH YOU?
YEAH, OF COURSE!
和
EXCELLENT! I LOOK FORWARD TO EATING IT.
...
I'M DEFINITELY CORRECT HERE... DEFINITELY ...
WOOSH

WHAT AN EL-EGANT TASTE.
RIGHT?
YES! THIS IS GOOD! SO THIS IS DAIFUKU!

NOM
NOM

I'M OUT OF SHAPE FROM ALWAYS WORKING IN THE FIELD.
KRK
KRK

LET'S GET STARTED WHEN WE'RE DONE EATING!
ALL RIGHT!
PLEASE GIVE US A MOMENT. YOU MUST TAKE A LOOOOONG TIME TO ENJOY A FINE MEAL.
KRK

YOU'RE GOING TO GIVE ME A MORE ADVANCED LESSON TODAY, RIGHT?

I GOTTA START OVER AGAIN FROM BASICS...?
AW, MAN...

PAT
PAT
SST
SLOW AND STEADY WINS THE RACE.
CONSIS-TENCY IS WHAT'LL MAKE YOU STRONGER IN THE END.

YOU KNOW WHAT I'M TALKING ABOUT...
COME ON, DON'T FOOL AROUND!

WHAT?

WHAT'RE YOU TALKING ABOUT?
PROMISE?

BEFORE YOU GO, WE SHOULD TALK ABOUT THAT PROMISE WE MADE WITH THE LORD OF EVERYTHING.
WAIT, BEERUS!

...I REALLY AM GONNA TAKE THAT NAP.
NOW THAT I'M FULL...

I'M TALKING ABOUT THE FIGHTING TOURNAMENT ACROSS ALL THE UNIVERSES.

WE DON'T NEED TO DO SOMETHING LIKE THAT!
I WANNA SET A GOAL BEFORE I TRAIN. AT LEAST LET'S MAKE A SCHEDULE BEFORE YOU GO TO SLEEP!

HEY! BUT IT SOUNDS REALLY EXCITING. IT'S GOING TO DECIDE WHICH UNIVERSE IS REALLY THE STRONGEST!
FORGET THAT NONSENSE...

I'M NOT JOKING AROUND. DON'T BOTHER THE LORD OF EVERYTHING ANYMORE.
YOU FOOL!

LOOK! THE LORD OF EVERYTHING GAVE ME THIS SWITCH. I CAN SEE HIM ANYTIME WITH THIS. MAYBE I SHOULD GO ASK HIM.
SHF

YOU FOOL! DON'T GET CARRIED AWAY!
HIM? I DON'T THINK HE'S THAT BAD. LOOK AT HOW ADORABLE HIS FACE IS.
NO! THE LORD OF EVERY-THING HIMSELF IS WHAT'S SCARY.
IS SOME-ONE REALLY SCARY GONNA APPEAR??

I'M ONLY ASKING ABOUT THE TOUR-NA-MENT.
WHY?

I WOULDN'T RECOM-MEND THAT EITHER. YOU NEVER KNOW WHAT'LL HAPPEN WITH HIM.

ZENÔ-SAMA IS SURELY PURE OF HEART. BUT HIS PURENESS IS WHAT MAKES HIM SO SCARY!
YOU MUST BE VERY CAREFUL...

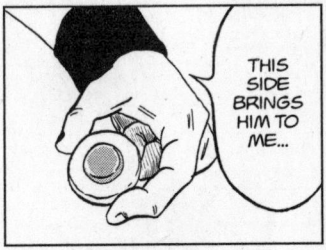
THIS SIDE BRINGS HIM TO ME...

WHICH ONE SHOULD I CHOOSE?
...AND THIS ONE TAKES ME TO HIM...
FLIP

I AM HIS FRIEND AFTER ALL.
IT'S JUST A TOURNA-MENT. IT'LL BE FINE.
DON'T GET COCKY!

PLEASE REMEM-BER THAT HE HAS THE POWER TO ANNIHI-LATE THE ENTIRE UNIVERSE.

KLIK
TOO LATE!
I'M TELLING YOU AGAIN-- DON'T PRESS THAT BUTTON!
REALLY, DON'T DO IT!
THIS IS DEFINITELY GONNA BE BAD!!!
THAT IDIOT...
FWIP
GOODNESS... HE REALLY DID IT!

...
REACTING BY ITS OWN WILL...
MMBL
BODY MOVES FASTER THAN MIND...
MMBL
SHWIP

DRAGON BALL SUPER

CHAPTER 28: THE GODS OF DESTRUCTION FROM ALL 12 UNIVERSES

ZENÔ-SAMA'S PALACE
CHECKMATE. UNIVERSE 7!
AH.
I ALSO HAVE FIVE MORE.
...
TAP
BUT I STILL HAVE FIVE MORE TO GO.
HMM ...

HEY, GRAND PRIEST. HOW ARE THE MORTALS IN THE 12 UNIVERSES DOING LATELY?
IT IS...
ISN'T THIS TOO MANY?
LET'S DO THAT.
WHY DON'T WE GET RID OF A FEW?
THERE HASN'T BEEN MUCH CHANGE WITH THE OTHER UNIVERSES... I WOULD SAY THE OVERALL LEVEL OF THE UNIVERSES MAY HAVE GONE DOWN SLIGHTLY.
UNIVERSE 1 IS IN THE LEAD, AS USUAL. UNIVERSE 12 IS NEXT WITH RECENT, RAPID GROWTH.
WOULD YOU LIKE TO GET RID OF A FEW?
I'M LOSING INTEREST IN OBSERVING THEM ALL.
SO AM I.
IT'S POINTLESS TO KEEP ALL 12 OF THEM.
IT IS.
SO, THEY'RE NOT DEVELOPING UP AT ALL.

THEN LET THE GUIDES IN THE DESIGNATED UNIVERSES WITHDRAW.
VERY WELL, MY LORD.
FWP
LET'S ERASE THE EIGHT UNIVERSES THAT ARE LOWER THAN THE OTHERS.
...
YOU'RE RIGHT. I GUESS FOUR IS GOOD ENOUGH.
...!

THAT WAS FAST!
OH, IT'S ZEN-CHAN'S HOUSE!

FWIP

OH, WE HAVE A GUEST.
MY LORDS, PLEASE HOLD ON A MOMENT.

WHO IS IT?
OH? WHO IS IT?

WHAT'S UP?! ZEN-CHANS.
WHAT DO YOU WANT?
APPARENTLY, HE WANTS TO ASK A FAVOR.
OH, GOKU!
I DON'T REMEMBER WHICH ONE OF YOU I PROMISED, BUT WE TALKED ABOUT THE INTERUNIVERSE TOURNAMENT BEFORE, RIGHT?
LOOKS LIKE YOU'RE BOTH GET-TING ALONG!
HOW'S EVERYTHING GOING WITH THAT? I'M TIRED OF WAITING.
YOU'RE RIGHT.
WE CAN'T DO THAT IF WE ERASE THEM.
THAT'S WHAT I THOUGHT.
AH, I FORGOT.

LET'S SEE. EACH UNIVERSE NEEDS TO PREPARE.
HOW ABOUT FIVE TIKS FROM NOW?
WHEN IS IT?
OH, THAT WAS FAST!
WHAT DO YOU THINK, GRAND PRIEST?
PLEASE DO NOT BE CONCERNED.
IT'S NOTHING.
HUH? WHAT'S UP?
THEN LET'S DO THAT SOON!

YOU ARE FROM THE PLANET CALLED EARTH IN UNIVERSE 7, RIGHT?
IN WHICH CASE, IT IS ABOUT 40 HOURS FROM NOW.
YEAH...
HOW LONG IS THAT EXACTLY?
HEY...
YES! LET'S DO IT!

SEE YOU!
OKAY! THANKS, I'D BETTER GO HOME AND PREPARE!

THAT SOON?!
FORTY HOURS?!

I MUST INFORM THE GODS OF DESTRUCTION, INCLUDING BEERUS. I NEED YOU TO STAY HERE AND WAIT.
HOLD ON A MOMENT.

FLASH
...
IT WILL ONLY TAKE A MOMENT.
FWOOP
BUT I GOTTA HURRY!
HUH?
THIS IS THE GRAND PRIEST. DO YOU READ ME?
ALL GUIDE ANGELS.

THIS IS...
...THE GRAND PRIEST ?

FLK
FLK

NOM
NOM

RCSTL
KLNK

HUH?
IT'S THE GRAND PRIEST.
FLK
FLK
IT IS YOU, LADY HELES.
WHO IS THE MOST BEAUTIFUL PERSON IN UNIVERSE 2?
FLK
FLK
E-EXCUSE ME, MY LADY.
I AM THE MOST BEAUTIFUL BEING IN ALL OF THE UNIVERSES !!
NO!

AND YOU WENT AND GOT HELP FROM BEERUS?!
SO, IT'S TRUE THAT THAT ZAMAS BASTARD WAS THE ONE WHO DID ALL OF THIS?
LORD RUMSSHI!
MY DEEPEST APOLOGIES...!

I JUST GOT A CALL FROM THE GRAND PRIEST!
OH MY ...

FLK
FLK
OF ALL THE GODS OF DESTRUCTION, HE IS THE ONE THAT I HATE THE MOST!!

!
WHAT DID YOU SAY?!

...
EFFECTS ON THE OTHER PLANETS IF THE PLANET'S BEEN DESTROYED... NONE.
POSSIBILITY OF HELPING THEMSELVES ...ZERO PERCENT.
FLK FLK
I'LL CALCULATE THE ODDS AGAIN JUST IN CASE...
THIS IS THE DUTY OF THE GOD OF DESTRUCTION.
THAT IS NOT POSSIBLE, LORD OF LORDS.
IS THERE REALLY NO OTHER CHANCE FOR THEM TO SURVIVE ...
I REGRET TO SAY THAT THIS PLANET IS SET TO BE DESTROYED.
...
IF I MAKE ANOTHER MISTAKE, THE GRAND PRIEST WILL GET ANGRY.
FROM THE GRAND PRIEST ?!
WHAT ?!
I'LL DEAL WITH IT LATER.
I AM WORKING ON A CALCULATION RIGHT NOW.
WE JUST RECEIVED A CALL FROM THE GRAND PRIEST.
LORD SIDRA.
MUR MUR

HERE YOU ARE, MY DEAR BELMOD.
OPEN WIDE.
HA HA!

TODAY IS THE ANNIVERSARY THAT MARKS 87,910,715 DAYS SINCE I BECAME THE GOD OF DESTRUCTION.
WE HAVE ENOUGH TIME. LET'S HAVE FUN UNTIL MORNING.

IT'S MY TURN.
NO FAIR!
OKAY, OKAY.

GULP

NOM NOM
YUP! THIS IS GOOD!

LORD BELMOD. THERE'S SOMETHING I NEED TO TELL YOU.

!
THIS IS...

YEAH!
FLK FLK
HA HA!

IRK
WHAT'S YOUR PROBLEM?!
HOW DARE YOU BARGE IN LIKE THIS!
DO YOU WANNA DIE?!
FLINCH
!
AH...
AGH...
FSH FSH
POOR THING... SHE WAS JUST AN INNOCENT GIRL.
HMPH... I WAS GOING TO DESTROY THIS PLANET ANYWAY.
E...
EEEEK !!!!
ANYWAY, WHAT'S WRONG, MARCARITA?
ARE WE IN A RUSH?
WE ARE.
VERY MUCH SO.

FLK
FLK
FLK
FLK
FLK

I ASSUME YOU ARE ALL LISTENING.
IS EVERYONE READY?

WILL THEY REALLY ALL COME OVER HERE JUST LIKE THAT?
HUH...?

LET'S WAIT A MINUTE.
THEY WILL.

THERE IS SOMETHING I NEED TO TELL YOU. I WANT ALL OF YOUR GODS OF DESTRUCTION AS WELL AS YOUR LORDS OF LORDS TO REPORT TO THE PALACE.
THAT'S ALL.

GOWAS!! I WILL CRUSH YOU TO DEATH!!!
IF THEY PUNISH ME FOR THE ZAMAS SITUATION...
SHOULD WE BRING A GIFT?!
THIS IS SERIOUS...
UNIVERSE 10
I DON'T THINK THIS IS--
NO WAY!
OH. THEY'RE ALREADY HERE?!
IT'S ABOUT TIME.
ZENÔ-SAMA'S PALACE
ONE MINUTE LATER
YES.
YES.
I'M READY.
YES.
PLEASE PROCEED.
ARE YOU READY, EVERYONE?

THEN YOU CAN COME WHEN HE'S DONE.
...
I APOLOGIZE.

MY LORD, GRAND PRIEST. THIS IS KORUN OF UNIVERSE 8.
MY APOLOGIES. MY GOD OF DESTRUCTION IS READY, BUT THE LORD OF LORDS JUST WENT TO USE THE REST-ROOM.

FWIP

NOW.
I SHALL CALL THEM IN.

OH!

SWF

SHOOOM

SHOOOM

W-WHAT...
WOOOOOOOOW!!!

THIS IS AMAZING!!!
THESE ARE THE GODS OF ALL THE UNIVERSES!!!

AN EMERGENCY CALL... HOW LONG HAS IT BEEN SINCE THE LAST ONE?
...
ROH
UNIVERSE 9
LORD OF LORDS
SIDRA
UNIVERSE 9
GOD OF DESTRUCTION
MOHITO
UNIVERSE 9
GUIDE ANGEL
LET US WAIT FOR THE ARRIVAL OF THOSE FROM UNIVERSE 8.
PLEASE RISE, LADIES AND GENTLEMEN.

WHAT'S GOING ON?
WAIT... THERE ARE TWO LORDS OF EVERYTHING...?!
PELL UNIVERSE 2 LORD OF LORDS
HELES UNIVERSE 2 GOD OF DESTRUCTION
SAWAR UNIVERSE 2 GUIDE ANGEL

SHIN UNIVERSE 7 LORD OF LORDS
BEERUS UNIVERSE 7 GOD OF DESTRUCTION
WHIS UNIVERSE 7 GUIDE ANGEL

IT'S BEEN A LONG TIME, EVERYONE.
AND FOR ME, IT'S NICE TO MEET YOU ALL!
HA HA HA!

G...
GOKU, YOU BAS-TARD ...!!!

WHAT'S YOUR MORTAL DOING HERE?!!!
HOW SHOULD I KNOW?!! DON'T ASK ME!!

HEY... BEE-RUS!!!

YOU'RE ALWAYS MAKING A MESS FOR THE REST OF US!
THAY GUY MUST'VE DONE SOMETHING AGAIN...!!
FUWA UNIVERSE 6 LORD OF LORDS
CHAMPA UNIVERSE 6 GOD OF DESTRUCTION
VADOS UNIVERSE 6 GUIDE ANGEL
BEERUS DID SOMETHING AGAIN...!
TCH...
KURU UNIVERSE 4 LORD OF LORDS
QUITELA UNIVERSE 4 GOD OF DESTRUCTION
CONIC UNIVERSE 4 GUIDE ANGEL
MAY I ASK YOU ABOUT THE GENTLEMAN BEHIND YOU?
MY LORD.
LORD BEL-MOD.
OH.
THIS MAN, MY LORD, IS TOPPO.

I AM TOPPO, AT YOUR SERVICE.

TO TELL YOU THE TRUTH, I AM PLANNING ON RETIRING ANY DAY NOW. I AM TRAINING HIM TO SUCCEED ME AS THE NEXT GOD OF DESTRUCTION. BECAUSE HE HAPPENED TO BE WITH ME, I BROUGHT HIM ALONG FOR THE EXPERIENCE.

PLEASE WORK HARD TO BECOME A GREAT GOD OF DESTRUCTION.
UNDERSTOOD.

M-MY SINCERE THANKS TO YOU FOR SUCH KIND WORDS.
TOPPO
UNIVERSE 11
CANDIDATE FOR GOD OF DESTRUCTION
KAI
UNIVERSE 11
LORD OF LORDS
BELMOD
UNIVERSE 11
GOD OF DESTRUCTION
MARCARITA
UNIVERSE 11
GUIDE ANGEL

NOW THEN... PLEASE COME.
SST

WE ARE READY NOW.
MY LORD, GRAND PRIEST.

FWIP
HA HA HA!!
ILLE
UNIVERSE 8
LORD OF LORDS
LIQUIIR
UNIVERSE 8
GOD OF DESTRUCTION
KORUN
UNIVERSE 8
GUIDE ANGEL
MY...MY APOLOGIES FOR KEEPING YOU WAITING!!
GULP
GULP
WELL THEN, THE LORD OF EVERYTHING HAS AN ANNOUNCEMENT.
EVERYONE'S NOW HERE.

HUH? TOURNAMENT OF POWER?
AGU UNIVERSE 12 LORD OF LORDS
GEENE UNIVERSE 12 GOD OF DESTRUCTION
MARTINNE UNIVERSE 12 GUIDE ANGEL
...WE HAVE DECIDED TO HOLD THE TOURNAMENT OF POWER– A TOURNAMENT IN WHICH THE CHOSEN FIGHTERS FROM EACH UNIVERSE WILL COMPETE.
I AM FULLY AWARE THAT THIS IS SUDDEN, BUT IN FIVE TIKS, PRECISELY AT 157 O'CLOCK, DAY 3,135,500,603 OF THE KING CALENDAR..
CHOSEN FIGHTERS... WHAT DO YOU MEAN...?
OGMA UNIVERSE 5 LORD OF LORDS
ARACK UNIVERSE 5 GOD OF DESTRUCTION
CUCATAIL UNIVERSE 5 GUIDE ANGEL
BEEP!
BEEP!
LORD MOSCO! YOU MUST NEVER SAY SUCH THINGS IN ZENÔ-SAMA'S PRESENCE!
...THAT IDIOT MADE ZENÔ-SAMA'S PLAN A REALITY...
JUST AS I THOUGHT ...
HE REALLY DID IT...

LORD OF LORDS FROM UNI-VERSE 3.
ARE YOU HAVING TROU-BLE THERE?
WHAT?
IT'S NOTH-ING, MY LORD!!
UM, NO!
SWF
WHAT DID HE JUST SAY?
EYRE
UNIVERSE 3
LORD OF LORDS
MOSCO
UNIVERSE 3
GOD OF DESTRUCTION
KAMPARI
UNIVERSE 3
GUIDE ANGEL
IS THAT BAD?
HUH?
LORD MOSCO WAS SIMPLY CONCERNED THAT WE HAVE SO LITTLE TIME TO PREPARE...
A-AS IT IS...
EVERY-THING IS ALL RIGHT, MY LORD.
AH! UH... NO!!

I KNEW THEY'D WANT IT TO BE AS SOON AS POSSIBLE !!
I KNEW IT.
LORD MOSCO NOW SAYS IT IS OUTSTANDING THAT WE CAN PARTICIPATE SO QUICKLY.
MUR MUR
HA HA HA...
AH...
IT'S SOMETIMES NECESSARY TO STRETCH THE TRUTH, MY DEAR LORD OF LORDS.
THAT WAS A CLOSE ONE...
YES.
AH, YOU MEAN THE TOURNAMENT OF POWER.
WHAT ?
HE SAYS HE DOESN'T UNDERSTAND WHAT'S GOING ON.
IS SOMETHING WRONG?
INDEED, ZENÔ-SAMA, WHO CAME FROM THE FUTURE, HAS NEVER SEEN ONE BEFORE.
I SEE.

ALL RIGHT!
WELL THEN...
LET US INITIATE A QUICK ZEN EXHIBITION MATCH, SHALL WE?
ALLOW ME TO SET UP A TOUR-NAMENT STAGE!
パチン
HUH? RIGHT NOW?
OH!
YOU MEAN RIGHT HERE?
OH!
FWIP

IT'S A STAGE ...!
TH...
THIS IS...

PLEASE ENTER THE STAGE.
NOW THEN, MY DEAR GODS OF DESTRUC-TION.

I GOT THROWN OVER HERE TOO!
YOU BA
TARD.
MANY
HAVE
YOU T
CAREFUL...
GOKU!!

WHAT?!!

HOLD ON A MOMENT. THIS TOURNAMENT OF POWER REQUIRES THE GODS OF DESTRUCTION TO PARTICIPATE AS WELL?
US...?! WHAT DO YOU MEAN...?!
GOWAS UNIVERSE 10 LORD OF LORDS
RUMSSHI UNIVERSE 10 GOD OF DESTRUCTION
KUSU UNIVERSE 10 GUIDE ANGEL

HOW SURPRISING FOR US GODS OF DESTRUCTION TO FIGHT EACH OTHER.
ANATO UNIVERSE 1 LORD OF LORDS
IWNE UNIVERSE 1 GOD OF DESTRUCTION
AWAMO UNIVERSE 1 GUIDE ANGEL
WOW, IS THIS FOR REAL?!!!
IT IS ONLY NATURAL THAT YOU WOULD BE REPRESENTATIVES IN THIS BATTLE.
YOU ARE EACH FROM DIFFERENT UNIVERSES...
HURRY UP.
RIGHT AWAY !!!
YES, MY LORD!!!
THIS IS BAD. I HAVEN'T TRAINED IN DECADES...
YES, YOU'VE BEEN AVOIDING IT.
THIS IS GETTING OUT OF HAND...
THUD
TAP
TAP

...SHALL BE TERMINATED, ACCORDING TO HIS MAJESTY.
THOSE WHO REFUSE TO GIVE IT THEIR ALL, BY THE WAY...
WHAT ARE THE RULES OF THIS FIGHT?
MY LORD, GRAND PRIEST ...
HE IS ALSO OFFERING A REWARD FOR THOSE WHO LAST UNTIL THE VERY END.
ZENÔ-SAMA WANTS TO PLAN OUT THE REST AFTER OBSERVING THIS BATTLE ROYALE.
HERE IT COMES...! THIS IS WHAT'S REALLY SCARY ABOUT ZENÔ-SAMA..
!!!

OH WELL. I GUESS IT COULD BE A GOOD OPPORTUNITY TO DECIDE WHO'S THE STRONGEST GOD OF DESTRUCTION, RIGHT, BEERUS?
I GOT IT...

I CAN'T LET MYSELF BE DE-STROYED IN A PLACE LIKE THIS...

THIS IS MAD-NESS!
HAVING THEM ALL FIGHT EACH OTHER AT ONCE...

QUITELA.
YOU'RE ALWAYS PICKING A FIGHT WITH ME, HUH?

WHO DO YOU THINK IS RE-SPONSIBLE FOR ALL THIS?!!!
GOKU !!!!
QUIT BEING SUCH AN IDIOT !!!

I'M NOT GONNA LOSE IN HAND-TO-HAND COM-BAT!!
I LOST TO YOU AT ARM WRES-TLING!!!
YOU LOST TO ME ONCE. WHY WILL YOU NEVER ACCEPT THAT I AM STRON-GER?

URK
GOOD LUCK, BEERUS!

UGH...

SO IT'S BECAUSE OF BEERUS'S UNIVERSE ...
OH GOODNESS, UNIVERSE 7 IS AT IT AGAIN.

IS HE THE REASON FOR ALL OF THIS?
THAT IS...A MORTAL FROM UNIVERSE 7?
CRAP...!

WELL, US GODS OF DESTRUCTION ALL HOLD A GRUDGE AGAINST YOU ANYWAY.
HEE HEE... YOU JUST DUG YOUR OWN GRAVE. NOW WE ALL KNOW WHO TO BEAT THE CRAP OUT OF FIRST.

IF I REMEMBER CORRECTLY, IN THE LAST EMERGENCY CALL, EVERY UNIVERSE WAS ON THE VERGE OF BEING ERASED, THANKS TO YOU.
DON'T TELL US YOU FORGOT ABOUT IT, MY FRIEND.

...

HUH?! HIDE-AND-SEEK?!
LONG AGO, WE HELD AN ALL-UNIVERSES INVITATIONAL HIDE-AND SEEK-TOURNAMENT. IT WAS ZENÔ-SAMA'S IDEA.
IT GOES BACK TO BEFORE YOU BECAME THE LORD OF LORDS.
WHAT HAPPENED BEFORE?

THE TOURNAMENT HAD TO BE CANCELED SINCE HE NEVER CAME OUT. HIS MAJESTY, WHO WAS TRULY ENJOYING THE EVENT, BECAME FURIOUS. IN ORDER TO CALM HIS ANGER, THE REST OF THE GODS FROM THE 11 OTHER UNIVERSES HAD TO MAKE EXTREMELY INTENSIVE EFFORTS TO PLEASE HIM. DUE TO THAT, THEY ALL HAVE ANIMOSITY TOWARD LORD BEERUS.
FOR THAT TOURNAMENT, LORD BEERUS WENT TO HIDE AND THEN FELL ASLEEP FOR OVER 50 YEARS.

WHAT... HOW COULD HE...
HE'S A TROUBLE-MAKER.

WELL, ASIDE FROM THAT, THERE APPEAR TO BE SOME PERSONAL GRUDGES TOO.

HA HA HA...
SOUNDS GOOD TO ME.
WHY DON'T WE START WITH BEERUS FIRST...?
TCH...
FWIP
FWIP
COME AND GET IT. I'LL TAKE YOU ALL DOWN AT ONCE.
HMPH! WHAT A BUNCH OF LOSERS! YOU CAN'T DO ANYTHING ON YOUR OWN.
THERE'S NO TIME TO WASTE!
NOW.
SHF
SHF
SHF
SHF

HERE STARTS THE ZEN EXHIBI-TION MATCH.
BEGIN!!!

FWOOSH
SWISH
FWIP
TAP
FWIP
FSSHHH
SHOOP

WHIS, WHAT'S GOING ON?

HE DODGED THEM ALL!!
WHAT'S GOING ON?! IT'S LIKE BEERUS HAS EYES IN THE BACK OF HIS HEAD!

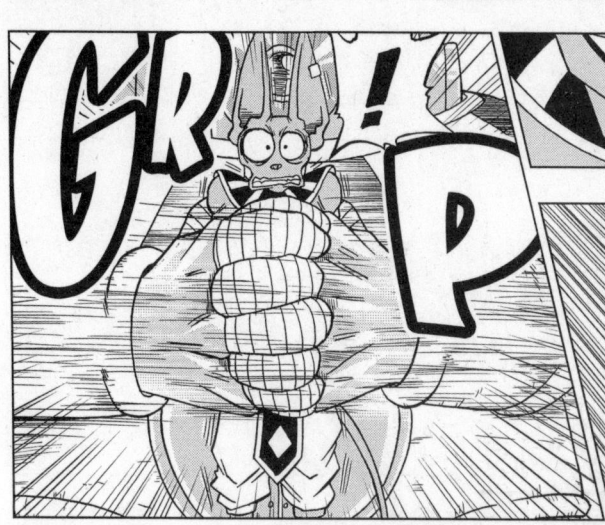
HIS BODY CAN SENSE ATTACKS AND CAN MAKE DECISIONS TO DODGE THEM.
GR!P

AH! THEY CAUGHT HIM.
EVEN LORD BEERUS ISN'T PERFECT ...

GAH!!!
SHF
SHF

NICE ONE, MOSCO!
HEE HEE ...
WOOSH
WOOSH
HMPH!!!
GWOOOOOOO
FWIP

BAM BAM BAM
BA
ABOVE US!!!
HE'S UP THERE !!!
SWF
TCH ...
THUD
WOOSH

!
THAT'S CHAMPA !!!
FWIP
!!
HA HA HA. THAT WAS BAIT, FOOLS.
THUD

YOU IDIOTS CAN STAY DOWN THERE.
EAT THIS!!!
BOOM

ARE THEY ALL STILL ALIVE AFTER THAT?
MAN... BEERUS ISN'T HOLDING BACK.
I SUPPOSE THEY ARE.
...
...
BOOM
!

HA HA. NO ONE CAN MATCH MY SPEED WHEN IT COMES TO BARRIERS...
SIDRA... YOU SAVED US ALL.
SHF
PHEW...
THEY HID BEHIND A BARRIER.

KRAK
THOOM
SIDRA!!!
UGH!!!

ONLY ONE OF US CAN BE AT THE TOP. YOU SHOULD KNOW WE DON'T HAVE THE LUXURY OF HELPING EACH OTHER.
IT'S NOT LIKE BEERUS IS THE ONLY ENEMY HERE, RIGHT?

BEL-MOD... YOU JERK!

I SAW TOO MANY OPEN-INGS TO HOLD BACK.
MY BAD.

TO BE CONTINUED!

A FEW DAYS AFTER BATTLING ZAMAS... HAVING LOST A FUTURE TO RETURN TO, TRUNKS IS PREPARING TO LIVE IN THE PRESENT...
THERE ARE PLENTY OF ROOMS HERE, SO PICK WHICHEVER ONE YOU LIKE.
THANKS.
YOU REALLY DON'T MIND ME LIVING HERE TOO?
BONUS STORY

!
THAT YOU, TRUNKS ?!

THANK YOU SO MUCH.
COOL. NOW WE CAN HANG OUT FOREVER.

NOT AT ALL! YOU'RE MORE THAN WEL-COME, IN FACT.
I'VE ONLY EVER HAD MY TRUNKS WITH ME, SO IT'LL BE GREAT HAVING YOU AROUND, KIND OF LIKE A DAUGHTER.

OH BOY, IT REALLY IS YOU!
WHY DIDN'T ANY-ONE TELL ME?

THAT MAKES SENSE.

WELL, I ACTUALLY STARTED TRAINING IN THE GRAVITY CHAMBER A LITTLE WHILE AGO. YOU SEE, THESE DAYS, NOBODY GIVES ME A CALL WHEN IT'S TIME TO FIGHT... FIGURED I SHOULD KEEP FROM GETTING RUSTY, JUST IN CASE.

G-GOHAN! WHY'RE YOU HERE?

IT'S GOHAN ALL GROWN UP! HE LOOKS JUST LIKE MY GOHAN, FROM THE FUTURE... LIKE HE'S BACK FROM THE DEAD.
THOUGH IT'S ALWAYS SO PEACEFUL AROUND HERE, SO MAYBE NO NEED? HA HA HA...
...

(APPEARED IN THE *JUMP VICTORY CARNIVAL OFFICIAL 2017 GUIDEBOOK*)

P9-CMX-049

YOU'RE READING THE WRONG WAY!

Dragon Ball Super reads from right to left, starting in the upper right corner. Japanese is read from right to left, meaning that action, sound effects, and word-balloon order are completely reversed from English order.